ABC

For JBY

QUENTIN BLAKE'S ABC
A RED FOX BOOK 0 09 943964 6

First published in Great Britain by Jonathan Cape,
an imprint of Random House Children's Books

Jonathan Cape edition published 1989
Red Fox edition published 2002

1 3 5 7 9 10 8 6 4 2

Red Fox Books are published by Random House Children's Books,
61-63 Uxbridge Road, London W5 5SA,
a division of The Random House Group Ltd,
in Australia by Random House Australia (Pty) Ltd,
20 Alfred Street, Milsons Point, Sydney, NSW 2061, Australia,
in New Zealand by Random House New Zealand Ltd,
18 Poland Road, Glenfield, Auckland 10, New Zealand,
and in South Africa by Random House (Pty) Ltd,
Endulini, 5A Jubilee Road, Parktown 2193, South Africa

THE RANDOM HOUSE GROUP Limited Reg. No. 954009
www.kidsatrandomhouse.co.uk

A CIP catalogue record for this book is available from the British Library.

Printed in Singapore by Tien Wah Press [PTE] Ltd

Quentin Blake's ABC

RED FOX

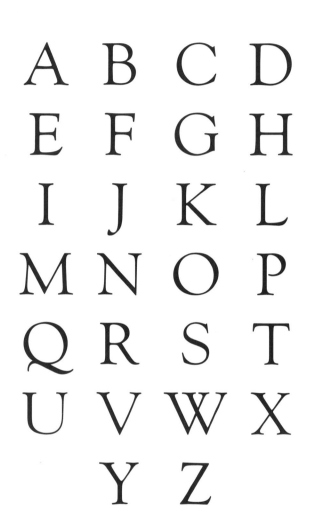

A B C D
E F G H
I J K L
M N O P
Q R S T
U V W X
Y Z

Aa

A is for Apples,
some green and some red

Bb

B is for Breakfast
we're having in bed

Cc

C is for Cockatoos
learning to scream

Dd

D is for Ducks
upside down in a stream

Ee

E is for Egg
in a nest in a bush

Ff

F is for Firework –
it goes BANG and WHOOSH

Gg

G is for Grandma –
she's really quite fat

Hh

H is for Hair
that goes under your hat.

Ii

I is for Illness
(which *nobody* likes)

Jj

J is for Junk –
rusty beds and old bikes

Kk

K is for Kittens,
all scratching the chair

Ll

L is for Legs
that we wave in the air

Mm

M is for Mud
   that we get on our knees

Nn

N is for Nose –
  and he's going to sneeze!

Oo

O is for Ostrich
who gives us a ride

Pp

P is for Parcel –
let's guess what's inside

Qq

Q is for Queen
   with a cloak and a crown

Rr

R is for Roller skates –
watch us fall down!

Ss

S is for Sisters,
   some short and some tall

Tt

T is for Tent
where there's room for us all

Uu

U is Umbrella
to keep off the rain

Vv

V is for Vet,
   when your pet has a pain

Ww

W is for Watch –
we can hear the ticktocks

Xx

X is the ending
for jack-in-the-boX

Y y

Y is for Yak –
he's our hairiest friend

Zz

Z is for Zippers,
That's all
That's the end

Other books by Quentin Blake